THE POETRY OF YTTRIUM

The Poetry of Yttrium

Walter the Educator™

SKB

Silent King Books a WhichHead Imprint

First Printing, 2023

"Earning a degree in chemistry changed my life!"
- Walter the Educator

dedicated to all the chemistry lovers, like myself, across the world

CONTENTS

WHY I CREATED THIS BOOK?

Creating a book about the chemical element Yttrium can be a valuable endeavor for several reasons. Firstly, Yttrium is a fascinating element with unique properties and applications. Its discovery and history are intriguing topics that can engage readers who are interested in science and chemistry. Additionally, Yttrium has diverse industrial uses, ranging from electronics to medical imaging, making it relevant to various fields. A book can provide a comprehensive exploration of Yttrium's properties, applications, and significance in scientific research. It can serve as a valuable resource for students, researchers, and anyone curious about the wonders of the periodic table.

ONE

OH YTTRIUM

In the depths of Earth's hidden embrace,
A secret lies, majestic and grace.
A shimmering element, rare and true,
Yttrium, oh Yttrium, we sing of you.
With atomic number thirty-nine,
In the periodic table, you define
A bridge between the elements, so grand,
A hero of the chemical land.
Your name, derived from a Swedish town,
Symbolizing strength and renown.
Yttria, where you were first found,
A treasure hidden beneath the ground.
Your electrons dance in an atomic shell,
A spectacle of beauty, we can tell.

From the depths of neodymium's fold,
You bring forth colors, vibrant and bold.
In lasers, you shine with radiant light,
A beacon of hope, piercing the night.
In alloys, you lend strength and might,
A foundation on which we take flight.
Yttrium, you hold secrets untold,
A mystery waiting to unfold.
In laboratories, minds will explore,
To fathom your wonders, forevermore.
Oh Yttrium, element divine,
In your presence, we find solace and shine.
A testament to nature's grand design,
Forever bound, in this poem of mine.

TWO

YET TO BE TOLD

In nature's grand design, a gem is found,
A rare and wondrous element, profound.
Yttrium, the bridge between earth and sky,
In its atomic heart, secrets lie.

From Yttria's town, where it first was seen,
Its journey of marvels began to glean.
A beacon of light, with colors so bright,
Yttrium, a symphony of vibrant delight.

In lasers it dances, with grace and finesse,
Its photons embrace, a celestial caress.
A catalyst of beams, a radiant source,
Yttrium's glow, a potent force.

In alloys it weaves, with strength and might,
A metallurgical symphony, shining so bright.

With iron and steel, it forms a bond,
Yttrium, a foundation, steadfast and strong.
Mysterious and enigmatic, its essence prevails,
In laboratories, where possibilities sail.
Scientists explore, with curious minds,
Yttrium's secrets, they tirelessly find.
Unveiling its mysteries, one by one,
Yttrium, a puzzle yet to be undone.
A guardian of elements, divine and rare,
Through its essence, nature's wonders we share.
So let us celebrate Yttrium's grace,
In the tapestry of elements, a treasured embrace.
For in its essence, the universe unfolds,
Yttrium, a story yet to be told.

THREE

PRECIOUS AND GOOD

In the realm of the periodic table,
A rare and majestic element resides,
Yttrium, the bridge between elements,
With grace and poise, it beautifully strides.
A shimmering gem in the atomic sea,
Its electrons dance, a cosmic ballet,
Symbol of Y, a symbol of unity,
Binding the elements in its elegant way.
Oh Yttrium, how you dazzle and gleam,
In lasers, you wield your radiant might,
With precision and power, you beam,
Illuminating the darkest of night.
In alloys, you lend strength and grace,
A secret ingredient, a hidden treasure,

Enhancing properties with your embrace,
Creating materials of untold measure.

Oh enigmatic Yttrium, mystery untold,
In your atomic core, secrets unfold,
Scientific exploration, your constant guide,
Unraveling the universe, side by side.

A tapestry of elements, woven with care,
Yttrium, you play your part with flair,
A symphony of particles, a cosmic dance,
In this grand creation, you hold your stance.

Yttrium, a name whispered in awe,
A story untold, yet to be understood,
In the vast expanse of nature's law,
You stand tall, precious and good.

FOUR

WONDERS OF YTTRIUM

In the atomic sea, a gem does shimmer,
A rare element, majestic and glimmer,
Yttrium, the bridge between elements,
With radiant light, it truly represents.
In lasers it dwells, a celestial glow,
Illuminating darkness, casting a show,
With energy it dances, in pulses and beams,
Yttrium, the star of laser dreams.
Alloys it adorns with strength and grace,
Binding elements, enhancing their embrace,
A hidden treasure within the blend,
Yttrium, the ally that will transcend.
Mysterious and enigmatic, it remains,
A puzzle to solve, its secrets it retains,

Through science's lens, we seek to unveil,
The wonders of Yttrium, the holy grail.

In the grand creation of elements, it stands,
A precious jewel crafted by cosmic hands,
Elegant and awe-inspiring, its grace,
Yttrium, the gem that lights up space.

FIVE

IGNITING SCIENTIFIC FIRE

In the realm of elements, a bridge doth Yttrium stand,
A conductor of change, a catalyst in hand.
With atomic number thirty-nine, it claims its throne,
A silent ruler in the realm of the unknown.
Yttrium, oh Yttrium, a silent enigma,
Mysterious and rare, a scientific enigma.
As lasers dance upon its surface, vibrant and bright,
Yttrium leads the way, a beacon in the night.
Alloys it does fashion, with strength and grace,
Melding elements together, in a seamless embrace.
From aerospace to medicine, it finds its place,
Yttrium, the building block, in this cosmic chase.
Its electrons dance, a symphony of light,
Unveiling secrets hidden, in the depths of the night.

With luminescence, it shines, casting shadows aside,
Yttrium, the illuminator, in this vast cosmic ride.

A precious gem, a treasure untold,
Yttrium, the rare, a marvel to behold.
In the tapestry of elements, it holds a special role,
Yttrium, the catalyst, that unites the whole.

So let us marvel at its elegance, its grand design,
Yttrium, the element, so rare and fine.
In laboratories and minds, let it inspire,
Yttrium, the bridge, igniting scientific fire.

SIX

MEDICINE TO TECHNOLOGY

In the realm of alloys, strong and bright,
There lies a treasure, a gleaming light.
Yttrium, the element, noble and rare,
With properties unique, beyond compare.
Within its core, a story unfolds,
Of strength and grace, its tale unfolds.
Mingling with metals, it forms a bond,
Creating alloys, resilient and strong.
In lasers it shines, a radiant beam,
Illuminating realms, a scientist's dream.
A master of wavelengths, it guides the way,
In realms of discovery, where mysteries lay.
Yttrium, a puzzle, a riddle to solve,
A secret it holds, that scientists revolve.

Uncovering its essence, with curious eyes,
Exploring its wonders, beneath the skies.
A silent guardian, it stands with might,
Uniting the elements, day and night.
Versatile and steadfast, in every role,
Yttrium, the element, that unites the whole.
From medicine to technology's advance,
Yttrium's touch, in every circumstance.
A beacon of knowledge, a guiding star,
Yttrium, the element, that shines afar.
Oh Yttrium, mysterious and grand,
In your presence, we truly understand,
The power of elements, united and true,
Forever grateful, for what you can do.

SEVEN

YTTRIUM'S GLOW

In the realm of elements, a radiant star,
Yttrium, the beacon, shines from afar.
A catalyst of light, an alloy's key,
A mystery unraveled, for all to see.
In lasers it dances, with brilliance untamed,
Its atoms align, as photons are aimed.
A symphony of colors, a spectacle rare,
Yttrium's brilliance, beyond compare.
From ancient lands, its name takes its birth,
Named after Ytterby, a place of great worth.
Yet still it remains, an enigma profound,
A puzzle unsolved, waiting to be found.
In laboratories, scientists explore,
Yttrium's secrets, they tirelessly adore.

Its properties profound, its uses vast,
A treasure trove of wonders, unsurpassed.

Oh, Yttrium, you grace the universe's stage,
As a building block, in nature's grand page.
A unifying force, among the elements' might,
Silent guardian, shining in the night.

So let us marvel, at Yttrium's glow,
A silent hero, we've come to know.
In alloys and lasers, in mysteries untold,
Yttrium, our companion, forever bold.

EIGHT

BRILLIANCE AND CLARITY

In the realm of alloys, a hidden gem,
Yttrium reigns with a silent hymn.
A catalyst of strength, it binds with grace,
A metal of wonder, in its rightful place.
With iron and aluminum, it forms a bond,
Creating a union, firm and strong.
Through heat and pressure, it withstands,
Forging a union that forever expands.
In the realm of lasers, it holds its might,
Yttrium dances in beams of light.
A luminescent glow, a mystical sight,
Guiding the way through the darkest night.
Mysterious and enigmatic, it remains,
A puzzle unsolved, a secret it maintains.

Its properties unique, its essence profound,
Yttrium, a treasure yet to be fully found.
    Oh Yttrium, element of allure,
A building block, steadfast and pure.
From alloys to lasers, you play your part,
In the symphony of science, a work of art.
    So let us marvel at your enticing glow,
As you guide us on a path we must go.
Yttrium, a symbol of endless possibility,
Forever shining with brilliance and clarity.

NINE

ENIGMATIC AND GRAND

In luminescent realms, where secrets lie,
There dwells a gleaming Yttrium, oh so spry.
With atomic strength and radiance bright,
It dances through the darkness, a celestial light.
A conductor of colors, a symphony of hues,
Yttrium, the alchemist, its magic it pursues.
In alloys it weaves, a tapestry profound,
Binding elements together, in harmony found.
In lasers it thrives, a beam of pure fire,
Cutting through the shadows, reaching higher.
With precision and focus, it guides the way,
Unveiling the mysteries of night and day.
Yet Yttrium, dear Yttrium, there's more to your tale,
A secret unknown, a riddle to unveil.

For in scientific realms, you hold the key,
To unlock the wonders of our curiosity.

In catalysts and ceramics, you whisper a clue,
A catalyst for progress, where dreams come true.
In magnetic wonders, you play your part,
Uniting forces, a symphony of art.

Oh Yttrium, enigmatic and grand,
You captivate our minds, forever we stand.
In laboratories and beyond, your essence will thrive,
A unifying force, in science we derive.

So let us celebrate, this element so rare,
Yttrium, the luminescent, beyond compare.
With each discovery, a new chapter unfurls,
A testament to your power, the wonders of this world.

TEN

FOREVER INSPIRES

In the realm of elements, a treasure lies,
A radiant force that lights up the skies.
Yttrium, the glowing gem so rare,
With secrets and wonders it's eager to share.
A beacon of brilliance, it enchants and enhances,
Alloys it enriches, their strength it advances.
A conductor of power, a conductor of light,
Yttrium, the luminary, shining so bright.
Its atomic dance, a mesmerizing sight,
Unveiling mysteries, revealing the light.
A catalyst it becomes, a unifying thread,
Binding the elements, where science is led.
In lasers it dances, a symphony of hues,
Awakening visions, igniting the muse.

In phosphors it glows, illuminating the night,
Creating a spectacle, a celestial delight.

Yttrium, the enigma, with elegance it reigns,
Unveiling the secrets, breaking through the chains.
A building block of wonders, a symbol of might,
Guiding our journey, through scientific flight.

Oh, Yttrium, the element of endless possibility,
A symbol of curiosity and scientific nobility.
In laboratories and minds, it forever inspires,
Unveiling the universe, fueling our desires.

So let us celebrate this element divine,
With its grand design and its power to shine.
Yttrium, the enigmatic force we adore,
Forever we'll seek, forever we'll explore.

ELEVEN

SCIENTIFIC ROMANCE

In shadows deep, where secrets hide,
A mystic element takes its stride.
Yttrium, elusive and enigmatic,
A building block, scientific and dramatic.
With atomic number thirty-nine,
It guides us on a quest divine.
A catalyst for progress and innovation,
Unveiling truths, sparking inspiration.
Luminescent rays, a celestial dance,
Yttrium's glow, a scientific romance.
Unlocking wonders, hidden from sight,
Illuminating the world with its brilliant light.
From lasers to alloys, its beauty is seen,
A symphony of elements, a harmonious dream.

Yttrium's power, a force to unite,
Creating art, an ethereal sight.
Its elegance, unmatched and rare,
Ignites curiosity, a cosmic affair.
A puzzle piece, in nature's grand design,
Revealing secrets, profound and fine.
Oh Yttrium, with your allure so pure,
A key to knowledge, forever secure.
In laboratories, your essence thrives,
A beacon of discovery, where science thrives.
So let us marvel at your atomic grace,
Yttrium, the element, we embrace.
Unveiling the universe, with every spark,
Forever guiding us through the dark.

TWELVE

FOREVERMORE

In the realm of elements, a mystery untold,
Yttrium, a jewel, its secrets unfold.
With atomic number thirty-nine it stands,
A luminescent glow in its magical hands.
Oh, Yttrium, a catalyst, a force so grand,
In ceramics and alloys, you firmly command.
Uniting forces, binding them tight,
Creating wonders, igniting the night.
A building block, a foundation of might,
In scientific realms, you shine so bright.
From lasers to magnets, you pave the way,
Unleashing progress with every new day.
Curiosity sparked, exploration inspired,
In the realms of science, you never tire.
A guiding force, elegant and pure,
Unlocking wonders, forever endure.

Oh, Yttrium, an artist's delight,
Etching beauty in alloys, a breathtaking sight.
In colors and hues, your essence appears,
Creating masterpieces, erasing all fears.

A symbol of power, a symbol of grace,
Yttrium, you hold the universe in embrace.
As we delve deep into your enigmatic core,
We're captivated by your allure forevermore.

THIRTEEN

AWE OF YOUR MAJESTY

In the realm of scientific progress, a jewel gleams,
A radiant element that unlocks the universe's dreams.
Yttrium, elegant and rare, a dancer in the atomic ballet,
Enchanting minds with its captivating display.

With steadfast grace, it binds elements in its embrace,
Creating alloys, forging new paths in space.
A conductor of light, it paints the spectrum with hues,
Revealing the secrets that the cosmos imbues.

Yttrium, the bridge that unites the worlds apart,
A catalyst for innovation, a beacon in the dark.
In laboratories, its wonders are explored,
Unveiling the mysteries, leaving scientists awed.

From lasers to superconductors, it paves the way,
Pushing boundaries, leading us into a new day.
With each discovery, a symphony of awe,
Yttrium, the maestro, conducting nature's grand score.

Oh, Yttrium, your allure is hard to resist,
A spark of curiosity, a scientist's tryst.
Through your atomic dance, we glimpse the sublime,
Unleashing the wonders of space and time.

So let us celebrate this element divine,
Yttrium, the catalyst that makes us shine.
In laboratories and observatories, we'll forever be,
Exploring, discovering, in awe of your majesty.

FOURTEEN

FUELING INNOVATION

In the realm of science, Yttrium stands tall,
A treasure of the periodic table, above all.
With atomic number thirty-nine, it gleams,
Unleashing wonders beyond our wildest dreams.
Yttrium, a catalyst of scientific progress,
Igniting curiosity, an eternal caress.
Its valiant electrons dance in harmony,
Creating pathways to endless discovery.
With its rare earth nature, it binds and unites,
An elegant force, shining through the nights.
Like a conductor, orchestrating the symphony,
Yttrium blends elements, forging unity.
In laboratories, its secrets unfold,
Unlocking mysteries, untold and bold.

From lasers to LEDs, it lights the way,
Illuminating our world, both night and day.

In superconductors, it defies the norm,
Conducting electrons with a magical form.
Magnetic fields surrender, resistance erased,
Yttrium's power, in science, embraced.

Yttrium, a gem, in medicine's embrace,
Radiating hope, with its healing grace.
From MRI machines to cancer therapy,
It saves lives, with unwavering efficacy.

Oh, Yttrium, a marvel, a scientific treasure,
Fueling innovation, beyond measure.
In chemistry, physics, and all that we explore,
You inspire us, forevermore.

FIFTEEN

STRENGTH AND GRACE

In the realm of curiosity's embrace,
There lies a secret, a wondrous trace,
Yttrium, an element, rare and grand,
Unlocks the wonders, at science's hand.
A catalyst, it sparks the flame,
In reactions, where mystery untamed,
Transforms the ordinary, with its might,
Yttrium's presence, a guiding light.
In ceramics, it paints a vibrant hue,
With strength and grace, it breaks anew,
Melding art and science, hand in hand,
Yttrium's touch, a masterpiece unplanned.
Magnets dance in harmony's delight,
With Yttrium's pull, a force so bright,

Aligning particles, in unison they sway,
Unlocking secrets, in science's ballet.

Oh, Yttrium, luminescent and rare,
A beacon of hope, beyond compare,
In labs and halls, it guides our quest,
To explore the unknown, with endless zest.

A symphony of atoms, it conducts with grace,
Pushing boundaries, in nature's grand embrace,
Illuminating the world, with its radiant glow,
Yttrium, a treasure, that science will forever know.

So, let us celebrate this element's might,
As it fuels innovation, like a star in flight,
Yttrium, a testament, to curiosity's reign,
Inspiring us, in fields of study, to forever remain.

SIXTEEN

NUMBER 39

In the realm of elements, radiant and rare,
There lies a gem, Yttrium, beyond compare.
With atomic number 39, it gleams,
A harbinger of wonders, it seems.
Yttrium, the catalyst of scientific exploration,
Unveiling secrets with profound revelation.
Its power, elegant and subtle, yet profound,
Unleashing knowledge, mysteries unbound.
With its magnetic allure, it captivates the mind,
Drawing scientists, curious and kind.
In laboratories, its secrets unfold,
A symphony of discovery, never old.
Yttrium, the artist's brush and palette,
Uniting elements, the alchemist's valet.

Creating hues, vibrant and divine,
The masterpiece of creation, it does define.
In medicine, it holds the key,
Unlocking cures, setting us free.
Radiation therapy, a gift it bestows,
Saving lives, where hope once froze.
In technology's realm, it takes its stance,
Fueling innovation, advancing the dance.
From lasers to superconductors, it lends its might,
Pushing boundaries, illuminating the night.
Yttrium, the element of progress and grace,
A symbol of potential, in every space.
Mysterious and alluring, it lights our way,
Guiding us forward, to a brighter day.

SEVENTEEN

SCREENS TO LASERS

In the realm of elements, one shines bright,
With elegance and grace, a captivating light,
Yttrium, the name that echoes in the air,
A symbol of progress, a scientific affair.
From the depths of Earth, it emerges with pride,
A secret of nature, forever to confide,
Its atomic dance, a symphony of might,
Unveiling mysteries, like stars in the night.
Yttrium, the catalyst of discovery's quest,
Guiding scientists to breakthroughs, their very best,
In labs and equations, its power unveiled,
A key to knowledge, forever hailed.
In medicine's embrace, it finds its place,
Healing ailments, with grace and trace,

A guardian of health, a remedy's guide,
Yttrium, the cure, we cannot hide.

In technology's realm, it sparks innovation,
Fueling progress, with boundless inspiration,
From screens to lasers, its touch divine,
Yttrium, the pioneer, forever to shine.

In art's vibrant canvas, it paints dreams anew,
A palette of colors, so vibrant and true,
From fireworks' brilliance to gemstones' delight,
Yttrium, the artist's muse, illuminating the night.

Oh, Yttrium, element of wonder and might,
Your beauty and power, a celestial light,
Forever we'll marvel at your luminous grace,
A symbol of science, in this vast cosmic space.

EIGHTEEN

TRULY DIVINE

In the realm of science's vast array,
A shimmering element holds sway,
Yttrium, the beacon of mystery,
Unveiling secrets in its chemistry.
With atomic number thirty-nine,
It dances in the cosmic design,
From Earth's core to celestial spheres,
Yttrium's essence transcends all frontiers.
In labs it plays a crucial role,
A catalyst for discovery's toll,
In lasers, phosphors, and alloys refined,
Its presence, a spectacle, forever entwined.
Explorers seek its treasures rare,
In ores and minerals, it's found with care,

From Scandinavia to the rolling seas,
Yttrium whispers its enigmatic keys.
    Oh, Yttrium, a symbol of might,
Illuminating the darkest night,
Your luminescent beauty we adore,
A guiding star forevermore.
    So let us raise a toast to thee,
Yttrium, the harbinger of glee,
In the realm of science, you'll forever shine,
A catalyst for progress, truly divine.

NINETEEN

PROGRESS AND SHINE

In the realm of science, a marvel we find,
A shining star, with secrets entwined,
Yttrium, the element, so rare and pure,
Unleashing wonders, to forever endure.
In medicine's realm, where healing finds sway,
Yttrium's power, in radiation's array,
A beacon of hope, in therapy's might,
Guiding us through darkness, with radiant light.
In technology's realm, where progress takes flight,
Yttrium's prowess, reveals a dazzling sight,
From lasers to screens, in innovation we see,
Yttrium's touch, unlocking technology's key.
In art's vibrant realm, where colors collide,
Yttrium's essence, artists cannot hide,
From pigments to dyes, in hues so profound,
Yttrium's brush, paints beauty all around.

In exploration's realm, where wonders unfold,
Yttrium's presence, a tale yet untold,
From alloys to engines, in journeys we embark,
Yttrium's guidance, ignites our inner spark.

Oh, Yttrium, element of boundless might,
Your mysteries, like stars, forever ignite,
Fueling our minds, with curiosity's fire,
Unveiling the universe, our deepest desire.

So let us celebrate, this element divine,
Yttrium, the symbol, of progress and shine,
In science, in art, in all that we pursue,
Yttrium, we salute, for guiding us true.

TWENTY

ETERNAL APPLAUSE

In the realm of elements, rare and refined,
Lies Yttrium, a treasure, beautifully designed.
A catalyst of progress, it weaves its magic thread,
In fields of science, art, and all that lies ahead.
In medicine's embrace, Yttrium finds its place,
A beacon of hope in the healing race.
Radiopharmaceuticals, with precision and care,
Target tumors, ablaze with a healing flare.
In technology's realm, Yttrium takes flight,
A conductor of electrons, shining bright.
Superconductors, lasers, and screens so clear,
Yttrium's touch brings innovation near.
In the artist's hands, a masterpiece unfolds,
Yttrium's hues, a story yet untold.

From vibrant pigments to luminescent glow,
Yttrium's brushstrokes, an artistic show.
From space exploration to the depths of the sea,
Yttrium's influence, a wondrous key.
Engines roar and satellites soar,
Yttrium's power, forevermore.
Oh, Yttrium, element of wonder and awe,
Your contributions, an eternal applause.
A symbol of progress, inspiration, and might,
Yttrium, shining star, forever in our sight.

TWENTY-ONE

THE CONDUCTOR.

In the realm of elements, a gem does shine,
Yttrium, the conductor, so divine.
With electrons dancing, in perfect choreography,
Unleashing wonders, sparking innovation's spree.
In superconductors, its power is unveiled,
Defying resistance, a marvel unassailed.
Electric currents flow, unimpeded and free,
Unlocking secrets of science for all to see.
Oh Yttrium, the magician of the laser's glow,
Painting beams of light, with colors that bestow.
From medical marvels to dazzling displays,
A symphony of hues, in mesmerizing ways.
On screens, it ignites pixels, vibrant and bright,
A tapestry of images, a visual delight.

From cinema screens to smartphones in our hand,
Yttrium's touch, transforming how we understand.
In art, it's a muse, a creator's best friend,
From pigments to glazes, its beauty won't end.
With every brushstroke, a masterpiece unfurls,
Yttrium's presence, enchanting the art world.
And in the vast cosmos, where stars twinkle high,
Yttrium's journey reaches the depths of the sky.
Exploration's ally, fueling rockets to space,
Unveiling the mysteries of our celestial chase.
Oh Yttrium, beacon of progress and light,
A symbol of innovation, shining so bright.
From science to art, and all that lies in between,
Your presence brings beauty, a world so serene.

TWENTY-TWO

NAVIGATES THE STARS

In the realm of science, where wonders lie,
There exists a gem that catches the eye.
Yttrium, a name whispered in awe,
A catalyst for progress, its wonders we draw.
In medicine's domain, it holds its might,
Unlocking cures, a beacon of light.
With radiance it guides, a healing hand,
Fighting ailments, a hero in demand.
Technology's realm, where innovation thrives,
Yttrium dances, the spark that drives.
In lasers it shines, cutting through the night,
A symphony of possibilities, pure delight.
But beyond the lab, its beauty transcends,
An artist's muse, where inspiration blends.

From canvas to clay, its hues enchant,
Creating masterpieces, a stroke of Yttrium's grant.

And in the depths of space, where mysteries unfold,
Yttrium's presence, a story yet untold.
A celestial guide, it navigates the stars,
Revealing the universe, its wonders bizarre.

Yttrium, a treasure, a symphony of might,
A symbol of progress, a source of light.
In medicine, technology, art, and space,
Its legacy shines, leaving a lasting trace.

TWENTY-THREE

LEGACY CLEAR

In the realm of elements, shining and rare,
Dwells Yttrium, a catalyst beyond compare.
A conductor of discovery, it holds the key,
Unleashing the secrets of the unknown, setting them free.
In alloys it dances, a silent partner it plays,
Strengthening metals, in countless arrays.
With strength and resilience, it lends its might,
Forging connections, binding them tight.
A luminescent beauty, it holds in its core,
Radiating brilliance, forevermore.
In lasers it thrives, a beacon of light,
Guiding us forward, through the darkest night.
Yttrium, enigmatic, a mystery untold,
In scientific progress, its stories unfold.

From the depths of the Earth, to the farthest of skies,
It whispers its secrets, as it continues to rise.
    An artist's muse, it sparks creativity's flame,
Inspiring masterpieces, bearing its name.
In strokes of a brush, or notes of a song,
Yttrium's presence, forever strong.
    Technology's ally, space's faithful guide,
Yttrium propels us, with each stride.
Innovation and progress, its legacy clear,
Yttrium, a symbol we hold dear.
    So let us celebrate, this element profound,
Yttrium's influence, unbound.
From science to art, it intertwines,
A testament to human endeavor's grand designs.

TWENTY-FOUR

WONDER AND MIGHT

In realms of science, a catalyst for discovery,
Yttrium, the guiding star, shining endlessly.
With progress and shine, it leads the way,
Unveiling mysteries, in the light of day.

An element of might, boundless and true,
Yttrium's power, in all that it can do.
Conductor of electrons, conducting dreams,
Unleashing the spark, where innovation gleams.

An artistic muse, with colors so rare,
Yttrium's luminescence, beyond compare.
In pigments and glazes, its beauty unfolds,
Transforming canvases, with stories untold.

A beacon of progress, a light in the night,
Yttrium illuminates, with purest delight.
In lasers and superconductors, it finds its place,
Pushing boundaries, with its cosmic embrace.

Treasure of science, medicine, and more,
Yttrium's legacy, forever to adore.
In space exploration, it charts the unknown,
Guiding us forward, where dreams are sown.
Oh, Yttrium, element of wonder and might,
Your presence ignites, a celestial light.
With each discovery, a new chapter unfolds,
In the realms of science, where your story is told.

TWENTY-FIVE

YTTRIUM'S INFLUENCE

In the realm of atoms, a conductor supreme,
Yttrium, the element, with electrons it gleams.
With powers unseen, it weaves a magical spell,
Innovation and technology, it does compel.
A catalyst of progress, a harbinger of change,
Yttrium's reign, across fields it does range.
From lasers to alloys, it plays a vital role,
Empowering creations that capture the soul.
In screens that shimmer, with vibrant hues,
Yttrium phosphors paint a cosmic muse.
In pixels it dances, a symphony of light,
Guiding our visions, in the darkest of night.
Art and space exploration, it intertwines,
Yttrium's influence, a celestial design.

In brushstrokes of stardust, it captures the sky,
Inspiring the dreamers, who dare to fly high.

In laboratories, where science takes flight,
Yttrium whispers secrets, unlocking the light.
From superconductors to medical breakthroughs,
Its versatility shines, in every path it pursues.

Yttrium, oh element, with beauty untold,
A symbol of inspiration, a story to unfold.
In science and medicine, progress it imparts,
A beacon of hope, in our quest for the stars.

TWENTY-SIX

BEYOND COMPARE

In the realm where electrons dance,
A conductor bold takes its stance.
Yttrium, a name so rare and fine,
A beacon of innovation, it does shine.
In labs of science, it finds its place,
Unveiling secrets, unraveling space.
With lasers bright, it paints the sky,
Guiding the stars, as they soar on high.
In superconductors, its power resides,
Unlocking realms where magic resides.
Through icy realms, where currents flow,
Yttrium whispers secrets, only few know.
And in the world of art, it leaves its mark,
A touch of beauty, a vibrant spark.

Pigments and glazes, with hues profound,
Yttrium's touch, a masterpiece found.
From brush to canvas, its colors ignite,
Awakening passion, creativity's might.
Inspiring minds, it fuels the flame,
Yttrium, the muse, a legacy to claim.
In the tapestry of human endeavor,
Yttrium weaves its threads, forever.
A symbol of progress, innovation's crest,
With every discovery, it stands the test.
So let us celebrate this element rare,
Innovation's ally, beyond compare.
Yttrium, the conductor, the artist's muse,
From science to art, it leaves its clues.

TWENTY-SEVEN

ART TO SCIENCE

In the realm of elements, a gem I find,
Yttrium, a treasure, rare and refined.
With atomic might, it dances in space,
A beacon of light, in the cosmic embrace.
In the artist's hand, it weaves a spell,
A pigment of gold, a story to tell.
From ancient manuscripts to vibrant paints,
Yttrium's presence, a masterpiece it taints.
In the realm of science, it leads the way,
A catalyst for progress, day by day.
In lasers it shines, with precision and might,
Unleashing a future, bathed in its light.
In the depths of the Earth, where metals reside,
Yttrium emerges, a secret to hide.

It lends its strength to alloys, strong and true,
Forging the path to innovation anew.
In the vast expanse of space's grand stage,
Yttrium soars, an explorer in age.
Its use in rocket engines, a fiery delight,
Thrusting humanity to infinite height.
So let us rejoice, in Yttrium's grace,
A symbol of progress, in every embrace.
From art to science, it sets our hearts free,
Yttrium, the element of endless possibility.

TWENTY-EIGHT

ERASING ALL FEARS

In realms of art, where colors dance,
A luminescent, captivating trance,
Yttrium graces the painter's hand,
With hues that shimmer, as dreams expand.
From cerulean blues to fiery reds,
Yttrium's magic, passion it spreads,
A catalyst of pigments, vibrant and true,
Unleashing creativity, in every hue.
In technology's realm, where progress thrives,
Yttrium's presence, innovation derives,
Superconductors, lasers, and screens,
A symphony of wonders, where Yttrium gleams.
In space's vast expanse, where stars collide,
Yttrium guides explorers, side by side,

Igniting propulsion, fueling their flight,
Unveiling mysteries, in the darkest of night.
In science's domain, where knowledge unfolds,
Yttrium shines, its story untold,
Catalysts and alloys, it engineers,
Advancing medicine, erasing all fears.
Yttrium, a titan of elements rare,
With beauty and power beyond compare,
A symphony of progress, it orchestrates,
A legacy of wonder, it consecrates.
So let us celebrate, this element divine,
Yttrium's brilliance, forever will shine,
In art, technology, and science's embrace,
Yttrium's essence, leaves an indelible trace.

TWENTY-NINE

ENDLESS POSSIBILITY

In the realm of art, a radiant hue,
Yttrium, the element, comes shining through.
With pigments and glazes, it lends its hand,
Creating masterpieces, a magic so grand.
From cerulean skies to vibrant blooms,
Yttrium's touch brings colors to rooms.
A conductor of beauty, it paints the scene,
Awakening emotions, like an artist's dream.
In space exploration, it takes flight,
Guiding us through the vast expanse of night.
From rockets to satellites, it lights the way,
Unveiling mysteries in the cosmic ballet.
In science's realm, it paves the path,
Unlocking secrets with its scientific wrath.
A catalyst for progress, it breaks new ground,
Pushing the boundaries, where knowledge is found.

In medicine, it lends a healing hand,
With MRI machines, a technological band.
Diagnosing and treating, with precision and care,
Yttrium's influence, a lifeline we share.

Yttrium, a symbol of endless possibility,
Inspiring creativity, guiding humanity.
A beacon of hope, a conductor of light,
Innovation and progress, forever in sight.

So let us celebrate this element divine,
A symbol of greatness, a legacy that will shine.
Yttrium, we honor your boundless grace,
Forever inspiring the human race.

THIRTY

SCIENCE TO HEALTH

In the realm of elements, let us sing
Of Yttrium, a captivating thing.
With atomic number thirty-nine,
Its beauty and grace truly shine.
In art, it paints a vivid hue,
Adorning canvases, old and new.
From vibrant yellows to deep blues,
Yttrium's palette brings joy to muse.
To space it soars, a celestial guide,
In rocket engines, it does abide.
Propelling explorers to the stars,
Yttrium ignites their cosmic memoirs.
In science, it wields a potent might,
A catalyst for progress, shining bright.

Unlocking secrets, expanding our view,
Yttrium's presence forever anew.
    In medicine, it heals and mends,
A savior to lives, it gently tends.
With its radiance, it lights the way,
Yttrium leads us to a brighter day.
    Oh, Yttrium, your power we adore,
In alloys strong, you forever endure.
From art to space, science to health,
You inspire us to dream and delve.
    So let us celebrate this wondrous element,
Yttrium, our guide, forever resplendent.

THIRTY-ONE

FUTURISTIC SIGHT

In the realm of art and science's embrace,
A noble element emerges with grace,
Yttrium, the luminary of innovation,
Guides humanity towards exploration.
    A spark of light in the vast expanse,
Yttrium's presence, a cosmic dance,
In stars and nebulas, its atoms unfurl,
Igniting wonder in every corner of our world.
    In laboratories, minds ablaze,
Yttrium's secrets, they tirelessly chase,
From lasers to phosphors, its brilliance shines,
Illuminating discoveries, stretching the confines.
    A catalyst for progress, Yttrium's might,
Unleashes the power of human insight,

In medicine's realm, it finds its way,
As MRI's companion, leading the way.
With strength and resilience, it paves the path,
In superconductors, defying nature's wrath,
Empowering technologies, sleek and bright,
Yttrium, the harbinger of a futuristic sight.
From art to space, it leaves its mark,
Unleashing creativity, igniting a spark,
A symbol of endless possibility,
Yttrium, the beacon of our curiosity.
So let us celebrate this wondrous element,
That fuels our dreams, wherever they're sent,
Yttrium, the inspiration we hold dear,
Guiding us towards a future bright and clear.

THIRTY-TWO

ARTISTIC FEAST

In the realm of elements, a gem I find,
Yttrium, a treasure of a different kind.
Unveiling secrets, it holds the key,
To art, science, and technology.
In the artist's palette, it paints with grace,
Colors vibrant, in every hue and space.
A brushstroke of brilliance, a masterpiece,
Yttrium's presence, an artistic feast.
In labs, it whispers scientific tales,
Unraveling mysteries, pushing boundaries and trails.
A catalyst for progress, it ignites the fire,
Unleashing innovation, taking us higher.
In medicine, it heals with gentle touch,
A guardian in the realm of health and such.

Within the MRI's magnetic embrace,
Yttrium reveals, with utmost grace.
Its healing properties, a soothing balm,
Reviving spirits, bringing solace and calm.
A guiding light, through darkness it shines,
Yttrium's touch, a gift divine.
In technology's realm, it paves the way,
A conductor of change, with no delay.
Unlocking doors, opening new vistas,
Yttrium's power, a catalyst for inventors.
Endless possibilities, it beckons us forth,
A symbol of hope, of progress and worth.
Yttrium, oh noble element, we sing your praise,
A beacon of promise, guiding our future's blaze.

THIRTY-THREE

ECHOES THROUGH SPACE

In the realm of elements, a gem does reside,
A radiant presence, with secrets to confide,
Yttrium, a name that echoes through space,
Unveiling mysteries, at its own pace.
In lasers it dances, a conductor of light,
Guiding beams through darkness, shining so bright,
With precision and power, it forges a path,
Igniting a future, where possibilities amass.
Alloys it joins, with strength and might,
Enhancing their properties, gleaming in the light,
From engines that roar, to structures that soar,
Yttrium's touch, innovation does implore.
In rocket engines, it propels us to the sky,
A catalyst for progress, as we soar up high,

Exploring the cosmos, with wonder and awe,
Yttrium's presence, the universe does draw.

Medicine embraces it, a healer so pure,
Unlocking the secrets, with a touch so sure,
In science it shines, a symbol of progress,
Unveiling the unknown, as we strive to impress.

Artistry embraces its vibrant hue,
Infusing creations, with a magical view,
A palette of colors, a painter's delight,
Yttrium's essence, an artist's guiding light.

Yttrium, a marvel, in our earthly domain,
A beacon of hope, a catalyst for gain,
With each passing day, its power we embrace,
Forever in awe, of its celestial grace.

THIRTY-FOUR

DEAR ELEMENT

In the realm of science, Yttrium reigns,
A catalyst for progress, it proudly proclaims.
Symbol Y, atomic number 39,
Unveiling secrets, pushing boundaries divine.
With strength and resilience, it stands tall,
Unlocking the mysteries, breaking down the wall.
From lasers to alloys, its uses abound,
In labs and industries, its wonders are found.
In medicine's realm, Yttrium finds its place,
A healer of ailments, a saving grace.
Radiopharmaceuticals, curing with care,
Fighting diseases, a promise to bear.
In technology's sphere, Yttrium's at play,
Conductor of light, illuminating the way.

From LED screens to superconductors,
Its power and brilliance, nothing obstructs.
Oh, Yttrium, your presence inspires,
A symbol of hope, kindling fires.
In art and in space, your influence soars,
Inspiring the human spirit to explore.
From paintings to sculptures, creativity's muse,
Innovations in space, where dreams fuse.
You guide us toward a brighter tomorrow,
A world full of wonder, free of sorrow.
Yttrium, dear element, we sing your praise,
For the gifts you bring, our gratitude stays.
Resilient and powerful, you lead the way,
A beacon of possibility, forever to stay.

THIRTY-FIVE

YTTRIUM SHINES BRIGHT

In the realm of medicine, Yttrium shines bright,
A beacon of healing, a guiding light.
Its isotopes employed, with skill and grace,
To target tumors, to conquer their trace.
Within the body, its particles roam,
Seeking out cancer, their purpose to comb.
With precision, they strike, a surgical blow,
Destroying malignancy, letting health grow.
But Yttrium's prowess extends beyond,
To the realm of technology, it responds.
In lasers and LEDs, it finds its place,
Emitting a brilliance, a luminous embrace.
In televisions and computer screens,
Yttrium's phosphors create vibrant scenes.

With colors so vivid, they captivate,
A testament to Yttrium's power innate.

And in the world of art, Yttrium inspires,
Its magnetic allure, fueling creative fires.
In pigments and dyes, its presence is found,
Infusing paintings with hues profound.

Yttrium, a symbol of progress and might,
A catalyst for innovation, burning bright.
In medicine, technology, and artistic quest,
It embodies hope, a world truly blessed.

ABOUT THE AUTHOR

Walter the Educator is one of the pseudonyms for Walter Anderson. Formally educated in Chemistry, Business, and Education, he is an educator, an author, a diverse entrepreneur, and he is the son of a disabled war veteran. "Walter the Educator" shares his time between educating and creating. He holds interests and owns several creative projects that entertain, enlighten, enhance, and educate, hoping to inspire and motivate you.

Follow, find new works, and stay up to date
with Walter the Educator™
at WaltertheEducator.com

www.ingramcontent.com/pod-product-compliance
Lightning Source LLC
La Vergne TN
LVHW010602070526
838199LV00063BA/5052
* 9 7 9 8 8 6 9 0 4 2 9 3 4 *